Both

CLONING AND GENETIC ENGINEERING

Nicola Barber

W
FRANKLIN WATTS
LONDON•SYDNEY

First published in 2013 by Franklin Watts

Copyright © 2013 Arcturus Publishing Limited

Franklin Watts
338 Euston Road
London
NW1 3BH

Franklin Watts Australia
Level 17/207 Kent Street, Sydney, NSW 2000

Produced by Arcturus Publishing Limited,
26/27 Bickels Yard, 151–153 Bermondsey Street, London SE1 3HA

Editors: Nicola Barber and Joe Harris
Picture researcher: Nicola Barber
Designer: Ian Winton
With thanks to Dr Catherine Bale for reading the manuscript

Picture credits:
Corbis: cover left and 39 (Reuters), 15 (Najlah Feanny/Corbis SABA), 17 (Jeff Christensen/Reuters), 26 (Jorge Z. Pascual/epa), 36 (Shepherd Zhou/epa). Science Photo Library: 21 (James King-Holmes). Shutterstock: cover right (18percentgrey), title page and 31 (Vasiliy Koval), 7 (Felix Mizioznikov), 8 (yuris), 11 (BioMedical), 12 (Laurynas Mitrulevicius), 19 (BioMedical), 22 (pics721), 25 (Jaroslav74), 28 (Nico Bogaards), 33 (18percentgrey), 35 (gpeet), 40 (Promotive), 43 (Florelena).

British Library Cataloguing in Publication Data

Barber, Nicola.
    Cloning and genetic engineering. -- (Both sides of the story)
    1. Cloning--Moral and ethical aspects--Juvenile
    literature. 2. Genetic engineering--Moral and ethical
    aspects--Juvenile literature.
    I. Title II. Series III. Barber, Nicola.
    174.2-dc23

ISBN: 978 1 4451 0992 3

Franklin Watts is a division of Hachette Children's Books, an Hachette UK company.
www.hachette.co.uk

Printed in China

Supplier 03, Date 1012, Print Run 1694
SL002126EN

Contents

What is Genetic Engineering?

Genes are often called the 'building blocks' of life. They carry the information that controls how every living being on Earth lives and grows. The science of genetic engineering allows people to alter the structure of genes in humans, animals and plants. This technique was one of the most exciting breakthroughs of 20th-century science. Today, the possibilities opened up by genetic engineering are still being explored.

In genetic engineering (also called genetic modification) particular genes are manipulated, or transferred from one living thing to another for a specific purpose. This process produces a completely new set of genes. Cloning is a form of genetic engineering that produces exact copies – a clone is an organism that is an exact genetic copy of another.

Both genetic engineering and cloning have many different applications and are now widely used in medicine, industry and agriculture. The manipulation of genes by humans produces living things that would not occur naturally, for example plants that produce a specific drug (see page 30). For supporters of genetic engineering, developments in this science have opened up a world of possibilities for the future. But for its opponents, there are serious concerns about its safety, and about the moral rights and wrongs of 'tampering with nature'. Read on to find out about the arguments on both sides of this story.

Restructuring nature?

'[genetic engineering] … presents probably the largest ethical problem that science has ever had to face. Our morality up to now has been to go ahead without restriction to learn all that we can about nature. Restructuring nature was not part of the bargain…'

George Wald, US Nobel Prize-winning scientist, 1976

Correcting the book of life

'Once we have read the book of life, we will start writing in corrections. At first, these changes will be confined to the repair of genetic defects, like cystic fibrosis, and muscular dystrophy. These are controlled by single genes, and so are fairly easy to identify, and correct. Other qualities, such as intelligence, are probably controlled by a large number of genes. It will be much more difficult to find them, and work out the relations between them. Nevertheless, I am sure that during the next century, people will discover how to modify both intelligence, and instincts like aggression.'

Professor Stephen Hawking, Life in the Universe, *1996*

Twin boys have fun on a spinner at their local park. Identical twins are nature's 'clones' – they both come from the same original cell and both share the same genes.

History of genetic engineering

In a sense, genetic engineering goes back thousands of years. Throughout the centuries, people have chosen to breed from specific plants or animals with particularly desirable traits (characteristics). This process is called artificial selection. People chose animals that provided good meat, or plants that produced plenty of fruit, and by breeding from them gradually altered the genetic make-up of living things for human benefit.

The science of genetics

While early farmers appreciated the advantages of artificial selection, they did not know how the process worked. The science of genetics began in the 19th century when an Austrian monk called Gregor Mendel began a series of

Gregor Mendel experimented with garden pea plants to work out how characteristics such as flower colour and pea shape were passed on from one generation to the next.

experiments on garden peas. He wanted to find out how traits such as size and colour were passed on from parent to offspring. From his observations he was able to draw up laws about how characteristics are transmitted from one generation to the next. His work was continued in the 20th century. Scientists began to understand that in the nucleus of every cell, microscopic threadlike structures called chromosomes carry hereditary information. This information is held in units called genes.

How does it work?

Every living thing starts life as one fertilized cell, which contains all the genetic information needed for the organism to live and grow. The cell divides then divides again – and the division continues to build that organism. As each cell divides, the information contained in the cell's nucleus is copied and passed on. By the 1940s scientists knew that this copying was probably done by a chemical called deoxyribonucleic acid (DNA) that makes up the genes. But a major breakthrough in understanding came in 1953, when the structure of DNA was discovered (see panel).

Crick and Watson

In a laboratory in Cambridge University, UK, Francis Crick and James Watson worked out that DNA is made up of two strands, like the sides of a long ladder, but twisted round each other like a corkscrew. This shape is called a double helix. In between the two strands, the 'rungs' of the ladder are made from pairs of chemical substances called 'bases'. There are four bases: A (adenine), T (thymine), G (guanine) and C (cytosine).

Right or wrong?

In 1972, scientists successfully cut and joined DNA from two different species, then inserted the new genes into bacteria. In 1983, the first gene associated with a particular genetic disease (Huntington's disease) was located. Since the 1970s the speed with which this technology has advanced is utterly breathtaking. But for many people that is part of the problem. One of the biggest questions to be considered throughout this book is: just because we can transfer genes, is it right to do it?

Human Genome Project

Using Crick and Watson's model of DNA, scientists worked out that the sequence of the four different bases (A, T, G and C) creates a chemical 'code'. This code controls how the cell lives and grows. All genes are made up of these four bases, arranged in different ways and in different lengths. During the 1970s and '80s, scientists developed increasingly sophisticated techniques to identify genetic sequences. The idea for an international project to identify all the genes of human beings – known as the human genome – was suggested in the 1980s, and the project started in 1990.

Aims of the project

As the genes and sequences of the bases were identified, the aim of the Human Genome Project (HGP) was to store all of this information in databases and make it available for use, particularly by businesses. Information from the project has since been used in a wide variety of applications – in medicine, in agriculture, in industry and for DNA fingerprinting (identification of living things by their DNA). Many of these applications are discussed in this book. However, another very important part of the project was to address the ethical, legal and social issues that it threw up.

Who owns the information?

Who should have access to genetic information, and how should

Human genome facts

- human genes are in the form of 23 chromosomes, which under a powerful microscope are X-like structures

- there are approximately 3 billion (3,000 million) DNA base pairs that make up the human genome

- there are an estimated 20,000 to 25,000 genes in the human genome, although the exact number is still uncertain

- the Human Genome Project began in 1990 and was originally scheduled to end in 2005, but technological advances happened so quickly that it was completed two years earlier in 2003

it be used? One of the major areas of debate is over genetic testing. Thanks to the technology developed for the HGP, and information that links particular genes with specific conditions, it is now possible to test for genetic diseases. Genetic testing is a very powerful tool that can reveal much about an individual's health now and in the future. But who owns and controls this information? And how does someone cope with the knowledge that they are likely, some time in the future, to develop a life-threatening disease? The social and ethical issues of genetic testing are explored more fully on pages 22–3.

This computer image shows two X-shaped chromosomes, and the double helix shape of DNA. The DNA base pairs are colour-coded yellow and green, red and orange.

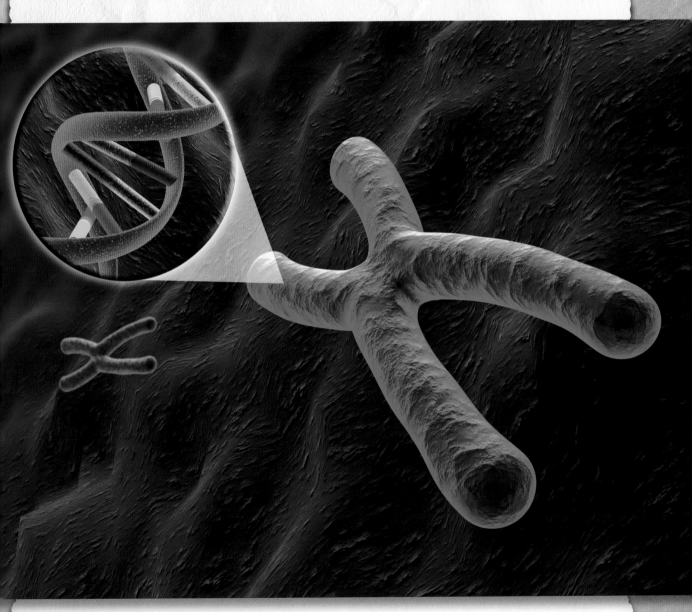

Transgenics

In genetic engineering, scientists change one or more of the bases to alter the sequence of a gene, or a set of genes. They can also move genes from one type of organism to another. A gene that is introduced into another organism is known as a transgene. If the transfer of the transgene is successful, the host organism begins to use the instructions contained in the new gene. In this way, scientists can introduce

Pigs, not monsters

'Somehow people think we are growing human arms out of the backs of pigs. Really, we are just looking at five or six genes. The pig still looks like a pig and behaves like a pig. We are not creating a monster.'

Philip O'Connell, director of transplantation at Westmead Hospital in Sydney, Australia, 2010

No discussion

'Biotechnology companies are breeding pigs with human genes in the hopes of fooling the human immune system into accepting a foreign organ from another species. This disturbing genetic reconstruction of life … is advancing on a commercial scale with almost no informed public discussion or effective oversight.'

From the website for the Campaign for Responsible Transplantation

new traits not normally found in a particular species (see pharming on pages 30–1).

Animal factories?

The science of transgenics raises many questions about the creation of new life forms, and the ethics of 'mixing' species together. Scientists have isolated the gene in spiders that controls the production of spider silk and inserted this gene into goats. The female transgenic goats grow up

(Opposite) A spider's web woven from spider silk. Spider silk is one of the toughest and lightest fibres in the natural world.

to produce milk that contains a spider-silk protein. The silk is then manufactured from the goats' milk. This artificial spider silk has many potential uses, for example it can be woven into ultra-light bullet-proof vests, or used in hospital surgery to sew up wounds. The benefits are obvious, but many people express concern that this technology reduces the host animals to little more than 'biofactories'.

Crossing boundaries

The technology of transgenic transfers from animals to humans is a major area of research, but also one of the most controversial. It is possible, for example, to use organs from pigs for transplant into humans, a procedure called xenotransplantation. The pigs are raised specifically for this purpose, and are genetically modified with human genes. But many people have serious doubts about the safety of xenotransplantation. There is a risk that a disease that normally only affects animals could be transferred into the human population. Many people also question the morality of crossing the boundary between one species and another in this way.

Cloning

The word 'cloning' is used to describe various different processes that are used to produce genetically identical copies of biological material. The most high-profile example of a clone was the creation of an entire mammal – Dolly the sheep – at the Roslin Institute in Edinburgh in 1996.

Reproductive cloning

The technique used to clone whole animals is known as reproductive cloning. It involves taking an adult somatic cell (any body cell except for egg or sperm) from an animal. The DNA from this cell is transferred into an egg that has had its own nucleus (and DNA) removed. This process is known as somatic cell nuclear transfer. The egg is allowed to develop into an embryo before being transferred into an adult female animal, where the embryo grows in the womb. If this process is successful, the animal that is born is a clone (identical genetic copy) of the animal from which the original cell was taken.

Dolly the sheep

The birth of Dolly the sheep was significant because she was the first mammal to be successfully cloned from an adult cell. As cells divide and multiply to create an

Back to life?

The possibilities opened up by reproductive cloning techniques have prompted some excitement about bringing long-extinct animals back to life. Body tissues from a few extinct animals, such as woolly mammoths, have been preserved in frozen conditions in the ground for thousands of years. Would it be possible to take cells from these tissues to create a clone? The challenges make this very unlikely – not least because reproductive cloning is a tricky technique with extremely low success rates, even in live animals.

Dolly the cloned sheep stands in her stall at the Roslin Institute in Edinburgh. Dolly's birth, in 1996, was a landmark in cloning history.

organism they all have the same DNA, but different cells take on different functions. Before Dolly, the majority of scientists believed that once cells had specialized into liver, or bone, or nerve cells, these changes were permanent. But Dolly was created from an udder cell taken from a six-year-old sheep. Her birth proved that cells are not 'fixed' in their function. This was a major breakthrough in our understanding of how cells work. While many people celebrated the birth of Dolly, others voiced their concerns. Dolly was created from a cell that was already six years old, and there was speculation that she might age prematurely as a result. In fact, she died at the age of six – about half the normal lifespan of a sheep of her type. After her death, scientists at the Roslin Institute stated that although she was suffering from lung disease, they had not found any abnormalities associated with premature ageing.

Animal and human cloning

The news about Dolly the sheep provoked great excitement about the possibilities for cloning in the future. Would scientists be able to clone endangered animals, favourite pets – even humans? What many people did not realize was the very low success rate of reproductive cloning. It took 277 attempts to produce Dolly. Some people also began to ask questions about this new genetic technology. What are the costs and the risks? How should it be controlled?

Endangered animals

The first endangered animal to be cloned was a guar (a type of Asian ox) in 2001. Sadly, the baby guar died only a few days after its birth. Since then other endangered species have been successfully cloned. However, many conservationists argue that dealing with other issues, such as loss of habitat or poaching, are far more important in the fight to save endangered species. They argue that cloning gives 'false hope' that some species can be saved.

Future technology

'The time will come when scientists will produce living versions of previously extinct animals … In some cases, it may be cheaper to save some DNA, and let a future, richer and perhaps more enthusiastic generation make its own copy of the species.'

Casey B. Mulligan, The New York Times, December 2011

Pushing the boundaries

What if you could clone your pet? In fact, it's been done. Both cat and dog clones have been produced, but at huge expense, and often suffering from deformities and other health problems. Opinion polls in the United States have shown that the majority of people strongly disapprove of the cloning of pets and endangered animals.

Similarly, experiments to clone humans are almost universally opposed and in most countries around the world are not permitted. The most likely use of cloning would be to help infertile couples to have their own children. But reproductive cloning is not a safe procedure and there would be great danger of miscarriages, or deformed babies. A clone child would be a 'copy' of its parent, a new type of human being, and no-one knows exactly what effect that would have. Would a cloned child be seen as a less unique individual? Or would it be similar to having a genetically identical twin?

Last-ditch measure

'Pushing future cloning technology instead of conservation is a terrible idea… cloning represent[s], at best, a last-ditch measure for saving traces of nature before it is gone.'

John Rennie, Smart Planet, December 2011

Two cloned kittens (left) are shown with the cat they were cloned from (right) at the Cat Show in New York, 2004. Although the kittens share their mother's DNA, they do not have her markings – these are determined by development in the womb rather than by genes.

Research cloning

Research cloning (also known as therapeutic or embryo cloning) is a technique that creates cloned embryos for research purposes. It uses exactly the same technique of somatic cell nuclear transfer (see page 14) as reproductive cloning. But instead of being implanted into a womb, the resulting embryo is used for the collection of stem cells. These are the cells produced during the first days of egg division, before the cells begin to take on different functions (see page 15). Harvesting the cells destroys the cloned embryo.

Stem cell therapy

Stem cells have the potential to develop into any of the roughly 200 different types of cell in the human body. Scientists hope that one day these cells may be used to 'grow' whole organs for transplant, or to replace damaged cells. This research could have a major impact on treatment of diseases such as multiple sclerosis, Alzheimer's or Parkinson's disease. But there are many challenges to overcome before stem cell therapy is a reality. Scientists need to work out how to make the stem cells develop into the correct 'replacement' cells, and how to get them to the affected part of the body. There is a danger that the stem cells might carry on dividing – causing cancer. And it is possible that if an infected stem cell was used to create more stem cells, many patients could be affected.

Pros and cons

So far, research cloning has only been successful using animal (rather than human) somatic cells. Human stem cells being used for research by scientists are obtained from embryos 'left over' after in vitro fertilization (IVF) treatment. This in itself is controversial, because many people argue that the embryo is a

So little value?

'...If the cloned human is of so little value at this early stage [the embryo], how could we ensure that he or she would be respected if allowed to grow to a later stage of development? ...Already a clone is perceived as a substandard, second-class human being.'

Comment On Reproductive Ethics (CORE)

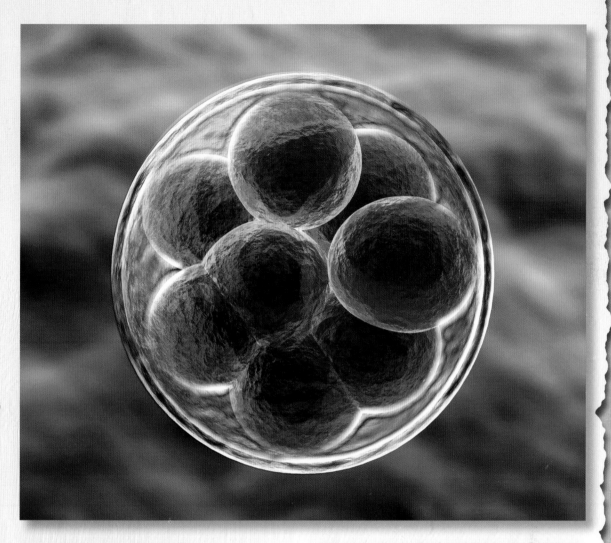

Three days after fertilization, this human embryo has eight cells. The process of dividing the chromosomes inside the nucleus of a cell into two identical sets, and two separate nuclei, is called mitosis.

human life, with human rights. They say that the destruction of embryos, whether cloned or not, is always wrong, regardless of the possible advantages. Another major objection to research cloning is that it potentially opens the door to human cloning, particularly in countries where regulation may not be very tight.

Need for research cloning

'In order to overcome the immune rejection problems associated with organ and tissue transplants, stem cells would have to be obtained from embryos produced from a patient's own cells, by means of research cloning.'

From the website of the Center for Genetics and Society

Genetic Engineering in Medicine

Almost every illness suffered by humans has some basis in our genes. But until recently, our knowledge about the role of genetics in disease was quite limited. Now, however, scientists, researchers and doctors have some powerful tools at their disposal. In particular, the Human Genome Project (HGP) has opened up new possibilities for the understanding and treatment of disease while at the same time raising many moral and ethical questions.

What is a genetic disease?

A genetic disease is the result of a mutation (change) in the DNA sequence of a gene. Some diseases, such as sickle cell anaemia, Huntington's disease and cystic fibrosis, are the result of a mutation in a single gene. These are quite rare. More common are diseases that are caused by small changes in a variety of genes in combination with other 'environmental' factors, for example a person's diet, or whether or not they smoke. Diabetes, cancer and heart disease all fall into this second category. Some genetic disorders are inherited, because the mutated DNA sequence can be passed on from parents to offspring.

Using the data

Genetics is playing an increasingly important role in the diagnosis and treatment of disease. The information

Textbook of medicine

'It [the HGP] is a ... textbook of medicine, with insights that will give health care providers immense new powers to treat, prevent and cure disease.'

Francis Collins, the director of the National Human Genome Research Institute, writing about the Human Genome Project in 2001

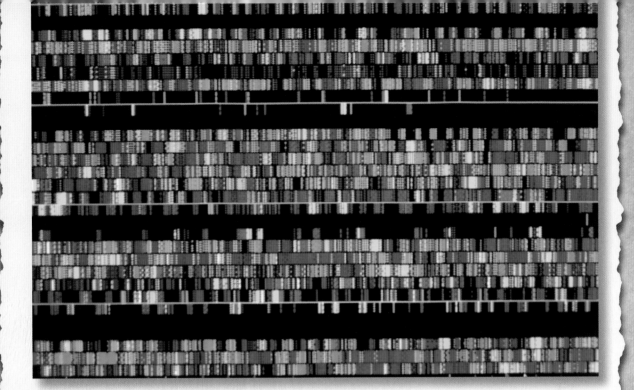

This computer screen display from the Human Genome Project shows the sequence of human DNA as a series of coloured bands. Each colour represents a specific base. The sequence of bases makes up the genetic code in the form of genes.

produced by the HGP is a vital tool for this work. However, it takes many years, and huge amounts of money, for biotechnology companies to go from raw data to a drug that is approved for use by patients. Other technologies, such as tests to diagnose symptoms or detect genetic abnormalities, are being more rapidly developed.

All of this new knowledge raises difficult questions. For example, a genetic screening test may show that a healthy person is at high risk of developing an illness in the future. But what if there is no effective treatment for that illness? And who should have access to that information? These and many other questions are the subject of this chapter.

New dilemmas

'Even when appropriate satisfactory laws and regulations are in place, there will still be many dilemmas ... What responsibility, for example, do individuals have to learn about their genetic makeups prior to their parenting of children?'

James Watson, in **New Perspectives Quarterly**, *2004*

Genetic testing

Genetic testing can be used to assess someone's risk of developing a disease in the future, long before any symptoms appear. But what are the implications for people identified as having an abnormal gene or genes?

Predictive testing

At the moment, predictive testing is usually offered to people who have a family history of genetic disorder. If the test finds no gene mutation, then the individual no longer has to worry about inheriting a genetic disorder. But often the information is not so clear cut. A person may have a gene mutation that increases the risk of breast cancer for example, but still never develop the disease. In other

Dangers of testing

'The presence of a gene associated with Alzheimer's disease should not be used to deny access to housing, employment, health care, insurance or any other goods and services.'

Alzheimer's Association, 2008

Need for testing

'Unfortunately, while there are over 1 million Americans that carry genetic mutations which dramatically increase their risk of developing cancer, fewer than one percent know it…'

Gregory C. Critchfield,
President of Myriad
Genetic Laboratories
in 2003

cases, a gene mutation means that the person will definitely develop the disease at some point in the future.

Helpful or unhelpful?

What do people do with this information? On the positive side, early detection may be very helpful for some diseases. There may be drugs or other preventative treatment that a person can take to delay the onset of the disease. Armed with information about their future health, people may choose to take steps to improve their lifestyles, for example by changing their diet, or exercising more frequently.

(Opposite) **Women take part in a charity walk in Chicago, USA, to raise funds for research into breast cancer. Genetic tests can now check for specific harmful mutations that increase the likelihood of developing this cancer.**

Others may use the information to make important choices about their lives, such as what career to follow, or whether or not to have a baby.

For some people, however, information from genetic testing may throw up more dilemmas than it solves. Does it help to know, for example, that you will definitely suffer from a disorder such as Huntington's disease later in life, when there is no cure for that disease? Tests may also reveal unexpected information which may cause great anxiety both to the individual, and to their family.

Who owns the information?

There is also the issue of privacy. If a person finds out that they have a genetic disorder which may also affect other members of their family, should they share this information? Should an employer or an insurance company have access to a person's genetic history? Many scientists and researchers fear that concerns over discrimination result in people being unwilling to come forward for genetic testing. In many countries, including the United States and in Europe, there are now laws that protect people against discrimination based on their genetic information when it comes to health insurance and employment.

Gene therapy

Gene therapy is the use of genes as 'medicine'. It involves inserting a gene or genes into an individual who is suffering from a genetic disorder. Sometimes the target of the healthy gene is to replace the mutated gene that is causing the disease. In other cases, the inserted gene has the effect of deactivating or 'knocking out' the mutated gene. This technology is still in its experimental stage, but it's possible that, in the future, gene therapy could take the place of drugs or surgery in the treatment of some diseases.

Is it worth it?

The failure of most clinical trials (see panel) has led many people to question whether the huge cost of research into gene therapy is justified. If gene therapy treatments are approved for use in the future, they will probably be very expensive. Who will have access to these treatments, and who will pay for them?

At the moment, research is focusing on inserting genes into somatic (rather than egg or sperm) cells. This means that the new genes would not be passed down to future generations. But, in the future, gene therapy could be applied to sperm or egg cells, meaning that its effects would be passed on from parent to child. How certain would we have to be that the procedure was absolutely safe before permitting such a permanent form of therapy?

Problems to be overcome

What are some of the problems to be overcome before gene therapy can be an effective treatment? One issue is that a gene cannot be directly injected into a cell – it needs some

Gene therapy trials

The history of gene therapy has not been straightforward. Gene therapy experiments on laboratory mice in the 1980s were encouraging, but those using human volunteers have been less successful. Since 1989, many thousands of people have taken part in clinical trials for gene therapy, but only a small number have had any success. In 1999, a volunteer in the United States died during a trial, and in 2003 two children developed cancer after receiving gene therapy treatment in France.

kind of 'carrier'. This is often a virus that has been 'deactivated' (made safe). But the body's immune system is programmed to fight foreign bodies such as viruses. Sometimes the immune system is effective at killing the virus before the inserted gene can take effect. There is also the potential risk that the virus may recover its ability to cause disease once it is inside the patient.

Another major issue is ensuring that the genes target the correct cells, and that these cells survive in the body. In many trials the inserted gene has stopped working after only a few days. The treatment needs to be long-lasting for gene therapy to be truly effective.

A laboratory mouse. Experiments on animals such as rats and mice are important in the development of new drugs and therapies.

Embryo testing

Many diseases caused by faulty genes can potentially be passed on from parent to child. But as our knowledge of inherited genetic disease has expanded, it has become possible to test embryos at a very early stage of development to find out whether they carry the faulty gene or not. This technique is known as pre-implantation genetic diagnosis (PGD). It makes use of IVF technology, in which eggs are removed from the woman and

Desired gender outcome

'Research and work carried out in the 1980's and 90's have finally provided methods offering the chance of obtaining a desired pregnancy gender outcome that ranges from excellent to virtually GUARANTEED.'

From the website of The Fertility Institutes, Los Angeles, USA, which offers a gender-selection service to potential parents

Blue or green eyes?

'If it gets to the point where we can decide which gene or combination of genes are responsible for blue eyes or blonde hair, what are you going to do with all those other embryos that turn out like me to be ginger with green eyes?'

Dr Gillian Lockwood,
UK fertility expert, 2009

sperm from the man, and the eggs are fertilized in the laboratory. The fertilized eggs are allowed to develop until they consist of around eight cells. At this point, one or two cells are removed and tested. Only embryos that do not have the faulty gene are implanted back into the woman. The others are allowed to perish.

Future possibilities

The main advantage of PGD is that if the pregnancy is successful, the couple know for certain that their baby will not suffer from the particular disease for which the

(Opposite) **Baby Roger, shown here with his parents, was born free of Huntington's disease in 2003, after pre-implantation genetic diagnosis.**

embryo was tested. In the future, this technology could potentially be used to eliminate some genetic disorders completely. Supporters of PGD consider that preventing disease is preferable to having to treat it.

Opponents point out many dangers, both practical and ethical. The techniques used to test embryos can easily damage them, and there is always the possibility that 'normal' embryos may be discarded alongside 'faulty' ones. And if it's acceptable to test for genetic disorders, why not screen embryos for less 'serious' faults, such as blindness or deafness? Some people fear that without tight regulation, such testing could allow parents to choose to have only 'perfect' children.

Male or female?

Embryo testing has already made it possible to allow parents to choose a male or female baby. In the UK this practice is illegal (except on medical grounds), but some clinics in the United States offer this service. Should parents be allowed to choose the gender of their baby? Many people worry about technology that allows people to choose any features of their future children.

Saviour siblings

At the age of 12 years, in 2011, Charlie Whitaker was given the all-clear by doctors to live a normal, healthy life. Charlie was born with an extremely rare form of blood disease caused by his bone marrow not making red blood cells. His treatment included regular blood transfusions and

No 'harvest baby'

'People would use the term "designer" or "harvest baby" to talk about Jamie, to make it sound like he was born for spare parts, but that is completely wrong. I really like the term saviour sibling because that is what he is.'

Mrs Whitaker, talking about her son Jamie (report from the Daily Telegraph*), 2011*

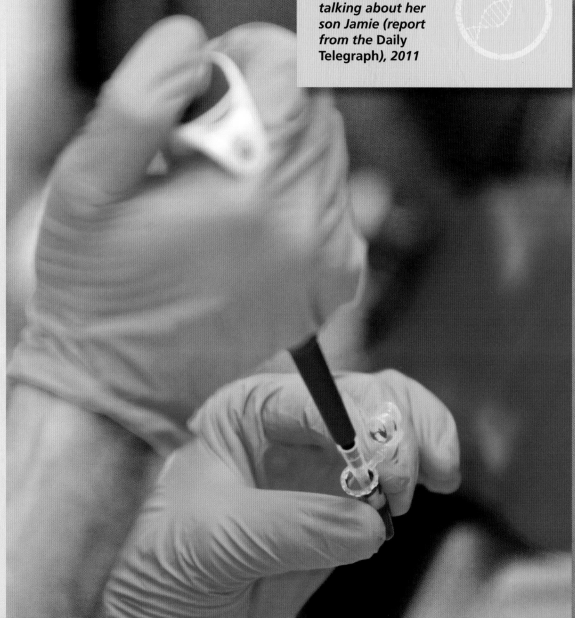

daily, painful injections. The only hope of a cure was a stem cell transplant. Stem cells have the ability to develop into many different types of cells (see page 18). Charlie needed stem cells that would replace his faulty bone marrow. Unfortunately neither his parents nor sister were a close enough genetic 'match' for the transplant.

Charlie's only hope was a 'saviour sibling' – a brother or sister specifically selected at embryo stage to be a genetically close match. After undergoing IVF treatment, Charlie's mother gave birth to Jamie in 2003. Stem cells were 'harvested' from his umbilical cord (the cord that connects mother and baby in the womb), and were used to replace Charlie's faulty bone marrow.

'Playing God'?

Charlie Whitaker's story is amazing. Many people will find nothing wrong in a family having a child who can help a brother or sister in this way. Others, however, ask if it's right to bring a baby

(Opposite) **Stem cell research: a laboratory worker uses a pipette to fill a test tube with stem cell culture – a liquid that contains nutrients to nourish and support the cells.**

Baby farming?

'… how will we prevent this eventually becoming a routine procedure, with thousands of babies being born as tissue donors for family members? As we contemplate such a scenario, expressions like "baby farming" come to mind.'

David King, Human Genetics Alert, 2003

into the world for the purpose of providing a treatment or cure for another child. What effect might this have on the 'saviour sibling' in the future? No matter how much they are loved by their parents, will they feel that they were born only to help an older brother or sister? Is this just another example of humans 'playing God'?

Such procedures have met strong resistance from organizations such as the Roman Catholic Church and pro-life (anti-abortion) groups. Many people in these groups believe that nothing can justify the testing, manipulation or destruction of embryos, even if another life is saved in the process.

Pharming

The word pharming comes from a mixture of 'farming' and 'pharmaceutical'. It is the production ('farming') of pharmaceuticals by genetically engineering plants and animals. Scientists insert DNA for a particular product into a host organism (a transgene; see page 12) that would not normally have that gene. The DNA is replicated in the host, which then produces the product.

High risk

'Some ideas, no matter how good they look on paper, should never be tried in practice. One of these is producing drugs or vaccines in genetically engineered food crops. The risk of these potent chemicals finding their way into the human food chain is just too high.'

New Scientist, 2005

Plant pharming

Scientists are experimenting with introducing genes into plants such as tobacco, potatoes, rice and tomatoes. The transgenes force the plants to produce proteins that are useless to the plant, but which can be collected from its leaves, seeds or roots and purified into drugs. The cost of producing drugs by pharming is potentially far lower than conventional methods of manufacture, and it is easy to 'grow' large quantities of drugs in a small area. There are also experiments to introduce human genes into plants such as bananas to produce edible vaccines. The transgenic banana plants produce fruits that contain the vaccine. They are easy and cheap to grow, can be eaten raw, and replace the need for expensive injections.

The most serious objection to pharmed crops is the danger of contaminating 'normal' crops. If these transgenic plants found their way into the food supply, people could potentially be exposed to uncontrolled amounts of drugs in their food. There are also concerns about assessing the effectiveness of pharmed drugs. For example, is an edible vaccine as effective as one delivered by injection, and how easy is it to ensure that each person has the correct dose of vaccine?

Animal pharming

Animals can be pharmed to produce medical products in their milk. The first drug from transgenic animals to be approved for human use (in 2006 in the European

Promising opportunity

'The advantages they [pharmed drugs] offer simply cannot be equalled by any other system. They provide the most promising opportunity open to us to supply low-cost drugs and vaccines to the developing world.'

Professor Julian Ma,
The Guardian, 2007

Union, 2009 in the United States) was an anti-clotting medicine. It is produced in the milk of transgenic goats. Opponents of animal pharming point out the need to keep these goats isolated to prevent their products entering the food supply. Many people also have deep misgivings about the use of animals as drug 'factories'.

A transgenic tobacco plant on a laboratory table. Transgenic plants have a wide range of potential uses, but are opposed by many people because of the risk of contamination of non-transgenic plants.

The future of medical treatment?

Doctors have long been aware that people respond very differently to medicines. A prescription painkiller may work well for one patient, but not for another. Lifestyle, diet and age all play a part in how people react to medicines. But increasingly, scientists are realizing that an individual's genetic make-up is just as important.

Pharmacogenetics (a combination of 'pharmacology' and 'genetics') is the study of how an individual's genes determine drug behaviour. Every person has very slight variations in their DNA which affect the way they react to drugs (see panel). By learning about these variations, it's possible to predict how effective a medicine will be in a particular patient.

Personalized medicine

Pharmacogenetics opens the door to 'personalized' medicine. Before prescribing any medicine, a doctor would run a simple DNA test on a patient to create a genetic profile. The profile would tell the doctor which medicines to avoid, and which would be likely to be most effective for that individual.

The promise of personalized medicine is that it will eliminate trial and error in prescribing drugs. A doctor will able to avoid a medicine that will cause side effects, or not be suited to a particular patient. It's estimated that around 100,000 patients die in the United States every year from adverse reactions to drugs, so this technology could make a real life-or-death difference. With better targeting of drugs, it would also be more cost-effective.

Your genetic profile

- the genes in your body contain the instructions for hundreds of thousands of different molecules called proteins

- some proteins determine the colour of your hair or eyes, while some of them metabolize (process) food or medicines

- slight variations in the human genetic code mean that some proteins work better or worse when they are metabolizing different types of drugs

Questions for the future

Critics of pharmacogenetics argue that research into this technology is very costly, and that funds may be better spent elsewhere.

Another potential problem could be the availability of drugs. A patient may have a condition for which there are only a small number of approved medicines. What happens

A doctor prepares a prescription for a patient – but how well will the patient respond to the treatment?

if you know from your genetic profile that none of the available drugs on the market are suitable for you? Equally, will drugs companies be willing to invest in research if they know from genetic profiling that a particular drug may only be suitable for a small proportion of the population?

Food and Farming

Genetic engineering is already used to modify both farm animals and crop plants. Some genetically modified (GM) animals are more productive than 'normal' farm animals; others grow more quickly, or are resistant to specific diseases. GM crop plants have been developed with many different traits, including weed and pest resistance, tolerance to drought or cold, and added nutrients (see page 37). The advantages of these modifications may seem obvious, but there are also many potential hazards. People from a wide range of viewpoints have raised concerns about genetic modification in farming and food.

The Beltsville pigs

In the 1980s, the United States Department of Agriculture funded the first experiments to genetically engineer farm animals. At the Beltsville Research Station in Maryland, USA, pigs were genetically modified with a human growth hormone. The aim was to create a faster-growing animal that produced less fatty meat. The result was a litter of piglets suffering from a range of conditions including damaged vision, ulcers and arthritis. Most of the pigs died before reaching one year of age.

'Frankenfish'?

At present there are no GM animals licensed for human consumption, but in the near future it's likely that genetically enhanced fish will be the first to receive the go-ahead for sale to the public. GM Atlantic salmon that grow twice as fast as wild Atlantic salmon have been developed by a company in Massachusetts, USA. After 20 years of research and development, the company believes that the fish pose little or no threat to the environment or human health. The GM salmon are kept in tanks on land, so there is little chance they will escape and mix with wild salmon. With wild fish stocks collapsing due to overfishing,

An angler shows off an Atlantic salmon before releasing it back into the river. GM salmon grow much more quickly than this wild salmon.

supporters of this technology argue that GM fish could help preserve the world's wildlife. They also believe that licensing GM fish – as well as meat from other GM animals – is vital to feed a rapidly growing human population.

Opponents of the GM salmon have nicknamed it 'Frankenfish' (referring to Mary Shelley's novel *Frankenstein*). They object to the conditions in which the fish are grown, which they say are cruel.

They have concerns about possible contamination of wild stocks, and they argue that there is little evidence to prove that eating GM fish is safe for humans. At the very least, if the GM salmon receive approval in the United States, opponents believe the salmon should be clearly labelled as a GM product.

GM animals and crops

As well as modifications to improve yield and growth, GM technology in animals is being used to develop disease resistance and to reduce animals' impact on the environment. For example, scientists have produced GM cattle that have increased resistance to 'mad cow disease' (an infectious disease in the brain of cattle). In Canada, a project nicknamed 'Enviropig' produces pigs that are modified to create less phosphorous in their urine and droppings. This could be good for the environment, since phosphorous from animal waste is a major pollutant once it reaches the world's rivers and oceans. But if Enviropigs were ever approved for people to eat, would they be good for human health?

A researcher checks GM rice seedlings at Huazhong Agricultural University, China, in 2011. China has given clearance for the sale of two rice varieties, both developed at the university, making China the first country to allow the commercial cultivation of GM rice.

GM for the future?

In 2011, GM crops were grown by around 16.7 million farmers in 29 different countries around the world. In the United States, the most common GM crops are soybeans, cotton and corn (maize). In Europe, GM corn is grown in six countries. This corn is modified to protect it from a common pest, the European corn borer, that can cause huge damage to crops. At present, no GM crops are grown commercially in the UK, although there are field trials taking place.

Many people argue that the use of GM crops is vital for the future of the world's growing population. They point out that a large proportion of GM crops are grown in the less-developed countries, where increased yields can make a real difference to people's livelihoods. For example, Bt cotton (see panel) has been grown commercially in India since 2002. Research has shown that farmers who grow this crop use less pesticide and spend less time checking their crops for pests. They hire more workers to pick the cotton, since the yield is higher. But opponents of this technology say that GM seeds are available only from a small number of global companies. This puts these companies in a very powerful and profitable position, because once farmers start to grow crops such as Bt cotton, they are usually obliged to buy GM seeds every year.

Examples of GM crops

added nutrients: 'golden' rice is modified to contain a higher than normal level of beta-carotene to correct low levels of vitamin A (a common cause of blindness)

herbicide-resistant: Roundup Ready soybeans are modified to withstand Roundup herbicides – this means farmers can spray their fields to get rid of weeds without affecting the soybean crop

pest-resistant: Bt cotton is modified to kill bollworms, a pest that attacks cotton plants (Bt stands for Bacillus thuringiensis, a bacteria that is found in soil and produces a poison that kills most insects)

salt-tolerant: GM tomato plants can be grown in fields where salt levels are too high for other crops – the plants take up the salt and store it in their leaves, but the tomatoes are unaffected

GM in our food

Surveys around the world about GM food crops have shown wide differences in public opinion. In the United States, there are no requirements for producers to label food packaging to say whether any of the ingredients are genetically modified. Research shows that most consumers in the United States know little about the extent to which their foods include genetically modified ingredients.

In Europe, attitudes to GM food have tended to be more hardline. In the UK, anti-GM demonstrations and strikes against trial GM crops took place in the late 1990s. Under European Union rules, all products that contain GM ingredients have to be labelled.

Risks and benefits

Two of the main arguments put forward by opponents of GM foods include accidental contamination and the risk of allergy. In 1998 a type of GM corn (called Starlink corn) was approved for animal or industrial use in the United States. It was not approved for human consumption because it was considered a high allergy risk. Scientists know that the introduction of a foreign gene or

Huge concerns

'For decades, public opinion polls have consistently shown opposition to GM, not least because huge concerns remain about the environmental impact of this technology, the risks associated with cross-contamination for the future of non-GM food, and the dangers of placing ever more control of food production in the hands of big GM corporations.'

Caroline Lucas,
leader of the Green
Party in the UK, 2012

genes into an organism creates new proteins that may not have been encountered by humans before. These proteins could trigger allergic reactions. In 2000, Starlink corn was detected in human foods, including taco shells. A few people reported being ill after eating the tacos, but tests did not produce any evidence to link their symptoms with the GM corn.

Supporters of GM foods argue that GM trials have shown no adverse health effects, and that GM foods are extensively tested before being approved for human consumption. They point out that GM foods have

Nothing to be scared of

'Opposition to GMs was perhaps understandable a decade ago, but today it is a mistake. The science is clear that genetic modification in food crops is nothing to be scared of, and in fact can help address numerous environmental challenges, such as the need to raise yields whilst using less water, pesticides and fertiliser.'

Mark Lynas, author and environmental activist, 2012

been eaten in the United States since 1996 without any widespread reported ill-effects. However, opponents of GM foods say that it is impossible to know exactly what effects they may have.

A protester takes part in a demonstration against genetically modified food in Montreal, Canada, in 2000.

Wider Uses of Genetic Engineering

The latest genetic engineering developments in medicine or agriculture often hit the headlines, but genetic modification has other applications that are less well-known. In warfare, genetic technology could be an extremely powerful weapon. In sport, genetic engineering offers new possibilities for athletes to be faster, stronger and better.

'Invisible' anthrax

Throughout history, people have used biological weapons in warfare. Early peoples used poisoned arrowtips to kill their enemies; today the technology

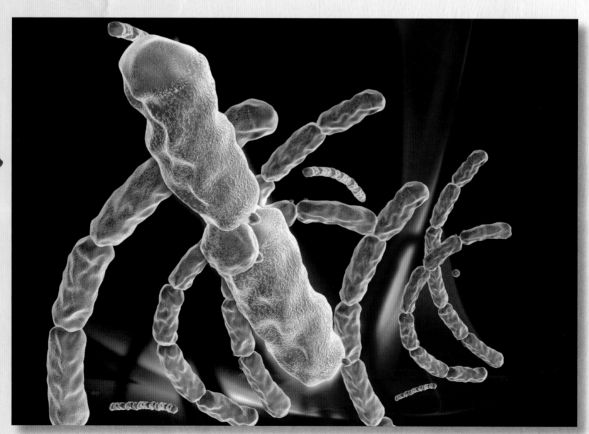

already exists to make highly sophisticated 'bioweapons'. In the 1990s, scientists from the former Soviet Union inserted genes into bacteria that cause anthrax – a lethal disease. The inserted genes altered the anthrax bacteria to make them difficult to detect. They also made the existing vaccines against anthrax ineffective. The scientists then engineered a new vaccine against the GM anthrax. This was important because, in theory, it would enable an army to vaccinate its own soldiers against this specific GM anthrax, while leaving enemy soldiers exposed.

Force for good or evil?

Since the 1990s, there have been rapid advances in genetic engineering technology. Developments in medicine and agriculture, as well as the knowledge uncovered by the Human Genome Project (see pages 10–11), all offer huge potential for improving the lives of people around the world. But exactly the same technology can also be put to use to create bioweapons. It may be possible, for example, to

(Opposite) A computer image of anthrax bacteria. The bacteria form spores (reproductive structures) that can be fatal if they are breathed in, or if they enter the bloodstream through a cut in the skin.

The smallpox virus

Smallpox is a highly infectious disease caused by the variola virus. It was eradicated in 1977 after a ten-year global campaign. Stocks of the virus were placed in two high-security laboratories in the United States and in Russia for research purposes. In recent years scientists have worked out the genome of the variola virus. This means that in the future it may be possible to recreate the virus from scratch in a laboratory.

manufacture GM weapons that will target specific groups of people based on the colour of their skins. Pharming (see pages 30–1) to create edible vaccines could be adapted to produce plants that would carry a gene to make people sterile (unable to have children).

Once the knowledge is available it is almost impossible to prevent such developments. But it is in the interests of everyone on the planet to use this technology for good. Because bioweapons are so powerful, work is ongoing on international agreements to control their research, production and use.

Sport

The latest scientific research is often applied to sport, but sometimes athletes and coaches are tempted to misuse such technology to try to gain an unfair advantage over their competitors. In the past this misuse has usually involved performance-enhancing drugs, a practice known as 'doping'. These drugs are almost all prescription medicines used to treat disease, which have a specific performance-boosting effect when taken by healthy athletes. In the future similar effects may be obtained through genetic engineering. The practice of inserting DNA for the purpose of enhancing athletic performance is called gene doping.

Gene doping

Doping in sport is illegal, and it is closely monitored and regulated by the World Anti-Doping Agency (WADA). In 2003, WADA added gene doping to its list of 'prohibited substances and methods'. One of the major concerns about gene doping is the high health risk to athletes. In many cases the technology is still experimental, and the results are unpredictable. But for some coaches or athletes, the promise of becoming stronger or faster than their competitors may tempt them to try gene doping, no matter how dangerous it may be. For the same reasons that it fights 'traditional' doping, WADA also considers gene doping to present a major threat to the 'integrity of sport'. They say that sporting competitions should be won or lost fairly through the dedication, skill and natural talent of the athlete.

The future of gene doping

Some people question WADA's approach to gene doping. They argue that genetic engineering potentially offers a safer way of enhancing sporting performance

Cheating and misuse

'The same kinds of people who cheat in sport today will probably try to find ways to misuse genetics tomorrow. Gene therapy has enormous potential to revolutionize medicine's approach to curing disease and improving the quality of life. Unfortunately, this same technology, like many others, can be abused to enhance athletic performance.'

Dick Pound, chairman of WADA, 2002

A safe and healthy way

'[genetic modification (GM)] is consistent with the values of elite sport. We expect world records to be broken and we thrive on witnessing increasingly extraordinary performances... where athletes are approaching their natural limits, GM offers a safe, healthy way of making such changes...'

Dr Andy Miah, in
The Independent, 2004

than 'normal' drugs. In the future, people may be born with some form of genetic modification. Will they be banned from athletic competition? What if genetic engineering techniques can be used to aid recovery from an injury – should this be allowed or banned?

Athletes of all types – from cyclists to long-jumpers – push their bodies to extremes. Is gene therapy a fair way to allow athletes to enhance the size and strength of muscles, for example, or to improve endurance by increasing the numbers of red blood cells in the bloodstream?

Glossary

allergy a reaction of the body's immune system to normally harmless substances in the environment

artificial selection the process of breeding from specific plants or animals with desirable traits

bacteria tiny, single-celled organisms that live in almost every environment on Earth

biotechnology the use of living organisms in engineering, medicine and technology

cancer a group of diseases all caused by the uncontrolled growth of cells that destroy normal cells

cell the basic unit of living organisms

chromosome one of the tiny X-like structures inside a cell that carry the genes

clinical trial a test of a potential treatment on humans to see if it should be approved for wider use

cloning a form of genetic engineering that produces exact copies (clones)

de-oxyribonucleic acid (DNA) the chemical that carries genetic information

embryo the early stage of development of a human or animal, in humans from the first cell division until about eight weeks after fertilization

gene a unit of hereditary information that occupies a fixed position on a chromosome

genome all the genes that make up a species

herbicide a substance used to kill unwanted plants (such as weeds)

hereditary something that is passed on through the genes from parent to offspring

hormone a chemical released by a cell or a gland that sends out messages to other parts of the organism

immune system the system in the body that protects against disease

in vitro fertilization (IVF) a medical procedure in which egg cells are fertilized outside the body and replaced in the womb

mutation a change

nucleus a structure in the centre of the cell that contains most of the cell's genetic material

nutrient a substance that an organism needs to live and grow

pesticide a substance used to kill insects or other pests that attack plants

reproductive cloning a technique used to clone whole organisms

research cloning (therapeutic or embryo cloning) a technique that creates cloned embryos for research

somatic cell any body cell except for the reproductive (egg or sperm) cells

species describes a group of organisms that share similar characteristics and can breed with each other

stem cell one of the cells produced just after fertilization, before the cells begin to take on different functions

trait a characteristic

transfusion the transfer of a substance (such as blood) from one organism to another

transgene a gene that is introduced into another organism

transplant the transfer of an organ from one organism to another

vaccine a weak version of a disease which is introduced into the body to stimulate the immune system, providing immunity against that disease in the future

virus a small infectious agent that divides inside the cells of living organisms

xenotransplantation the use of organs from one species for transplant into another

Further information

Books

Cells and Life: Genetic Engineering Robert Snedden, Heinemann, 2007

Cool Science: Genetic Engineering Ron Fridell, Lerner, 2008

Ethical Debates: Genetic Engineering Pete Moore, Wayland, 2007

Opposing Viewpoints: Cloning Greenhaven Press, 2012

Science at the Edge: Cloning Sally Morgan, Heinemann, 2009

Sci-Hi Science Issues: Should Scientists Pursue Cloning? Sally Morgan, Raintree, 2012

Websites

http://www.actionbioscience.org/
Action Bioscience website with a good section on genetics

http://www.clonesafety.org/
Website about cloning sponsored by several animal cloning and livestock genetics companies

http://www.geneticsandsociety.org/index.php
Center for Genetics and Society website

http://www.genome.gov/
The National Human Genome Research Institute has huge amounts of useful information about health, education and issues in genetics

http://genomics.energy.gov/
Gateway to the US Department of Energy's genomic websites

http://learn.genetics.utah.edu/
University of Utah website Learn.Genetics includes genes, cloning and gene therapy

http://www.roslin.ed.ac.uk/public-interest/dolly-the-sheep/
Information from the Roslin Institute about Dolly the sheep

http://stemcells.nih.gov/index.asp
Learn more about stem cells

http://www.wada-ama.org/en/
World Anti-Doping Agency website

Index

Bold entries indicate pictures